Original title:
Rhizome Rhymes

Copyright © 2025 Creative Arts Management OÜ
All rights reserved.

Author: Eleanor Prescott
ISBN HARDBACK: 978-1-80567-054-4
ISBN PAPERBACK: 978-1-80567-134-3

Patterns of the Profound

In a twisty world, roots dance and sway,
Chasing butterflies, they giggle all day.
Beneath the soil, secrets they weave,
Turning every plant into a jester's sleeve.

With laughter like rain, they splash and twirl,
Mischief unfolds in a leafy whirl.
Roots playing tag, what a sight to see!
Who knew that plants could be so free?

Beneath the Canopy

Under the leaves, where the shadows play,
Tiny critters laugh, come out to sway.
A snail in a top hat, oh what a show,
Twirling his shell in the sun's soft glow.

The moss wears sneakers, ready to race,
While ants in a band find their groove and grace.
Beneath the canopy, a silly parade,
Join in the fun, let worries be laid!

Unseen Footfalls

In the moonlit night, footsteps we hear,
But look twice, friend, it's just a deer!
They stumble and tumble, such clumsy sprites,
Leaving behind tales of silly delights.

A raccoon with manners tiptoes around,
On a quest for snacks he just might have found.
With giggles galore, the forest does sing,
Of unseen footfalls and the joy they bring.

Cultivating Dreams

Digging in dirt, the sprouts start to chat,
Planning great schemes, as only plants can.
A sunflower claims it's taller, no doubt,
While peas tease beans — what a playful bout!

With stars in their eyes and roots in the mud,
They plan to outgrow each little bud.
Fertilizer tales of grandeur unfold,
In a garden where dreams are bold and untold.

Syllables Underground

In the soil where whispers play,
Wiggly words have lost their way.
Dancing roots with silly glee,
Laughing bugs join in the spree.

Beneath the ground, the chatter hums,
Tickling toes where giggle comes.
Every sprout a punchline brings,
Sprouting jokes and quirky flings.

Sprigs of Thought

Little thoughts that twist and turn,
Bubbling minds with roots that churn.
Sprigs of wisdom, oh so bright,
Bouncing around in pure delight.

Nuts are cracking, laughter flies,
As ideas stretch to the skies.
Branches sway in silly fun,
Chasing shadows, one by one.

Branching Melodies

Tunes that flutter, leaves that sway,
Bouncing notes both night and day.
Harmony in every twist,
Even branches can't resist.

A chorus formed from roots and stems,
Jokes are woven in their hems.
Silly songs of growth and cheer,
Echo laughter far and near.

Silent Groves

In silent groves where shadows play,
Jokes are whispered, gone astray.
Branches chuckle, leaves all grin,
Nature's humor held within.

Tree trunks dancing, mossy feet,
Trippy tales of leafy meet.
Beneath the quiet, a jest lies,
Laughter hidden in disguise.

The Language of Shadows

In corners where whispers dare to creep,
Shadows make jokes, secrets they keep.
They dance on the walls, a comical flow,
Making us giggle, a shadowy show.

A wallflower's waltz, oh so absurd,
Rounded edges, not a single word.
Tickling the light, playing a game,
Who knew that shadows had such silly fame?

Threads of Existence

Spinning tales with fuzzy thread,
Socks that wandered off, it's said.
A mismatched dance under the bed,
Woolly yarns that are better off fled.

Knitting laughter into each seam,
Purling joy like a silly dream.
Tangled knots of our daily grind,
Who knew existence was so unrefined?

Nutrients of Narrative

Feeding stories like plants in bloom,
Watering tales with laughter in the room.
Compost of chaos, rich and absurd,
Sprouts of humor from each silly word.

Roots entwined in giggles and fun,
Photosynthesizing puns, a tasty run.
Harvesting smiles, oh, what a treat,
In this garden of gags, we all take a seat.

Echoing Earth

Beneath our feet, a giggly sound,
Mirthful echoes dance all around.
The ground chuckles, does a little jig,
A secret punchline, a playful dig.

Cracks in the pavement, stories unfold,
Where laughter's the treasure, pure, bright, and bold.
Nature's own stand-up, with roots all a-vibe,
Echoing joy, the earth's own tribe.

Botanical Ballads

In a garden where daisies dance,
A cactus tried to find romance.
It wore a hat, looked quite dapper,
But it pricked the heart of a happy sapper.

The roses giggled, feeling proud,
While tulips formed a silly crowd.
They twirled and spun, with laughter bright,
In a floral party under moonlight.

Beneath the Canopy

Underneath the mighty oak,
A squirrel croaked a funny joke.
The branches shook with laughter loud,
While hidden critters joined the crowd.

Mushrooms danced in a wild trance,
While sunlight twinkled, like a glance.
The leaves all rustled, 'Let's join in!'
As nature's joy began to spin.

Nature's Chorus

The bees all hummed a merry tune,
While fireflies sparkled like a boon.
A frog leaped high, to catch the beat,
And birds chirped loudly, oh what a feat!

Together they formed a vibrant song,
Where plant and critter just belong.
With each note, the flowers swayed,
In a symphony that nature played.

Sprouting Lines

A little seed had big dreams,
To sprout and find its sunlit beams.
But it tripped on roots along the way,
And laughed as it rolled in the hay.

With glee it popped, a sprout so spry,
It reached for clouds, oh my, oh my!
The flowers cheered, 'You did it right!'
And nature joined the joyous flight.

Elysian Underground

In the dirt, the giggles dwell,
Worms with jokes, they weave a spell.
Moles wearing hats, a sight to see,
Throwing a party, just for me!

Rabbits hop to chime the tune,
Underneath the silver moon.
Radishes dance, oh what a scene,
With carrots laughing, big and green!

A gopher juggles little stones,
While laughing bees buzz funny tones.
In this land below the grass,
Time flies quickly, oh what a pass!

With every root, a tale unfolds,
Laughter wraps in nature's folds.
In this spot, beneath the ground,
Joy and mischief can be found!

Weaving the Unseen Paths

Through tangled vines and leafy trails,
Squirrels tell silly, wacky tales.
The pinecone sings a comical song,
As mushrooms giggle, joining along!

A hedgehog spins a yarn so wild,
While rabbits hop like they're a child.
Dandelions burst in fits of cheer,
Whispering secrets for all to hear!

Worms in tuxedos stroll with pride,
Tickling each root on their slippery ride.
These hidden paths, so full of jest,
Invite us all to be a guest!

Underneath the shady trees,
The insects chuckle with the breeze.
At nature's party, join the fun,
And sprout a smile, my little one!

The Language of Leaves

Whispering leaves have tales to tell,
Of acorns bouncing, oh so well!
In every rustle, laughter's song,
Nature's chorus, dancing along.

The ferns are gossiping with flair,
While ladybugs twirl without a care.
In every shadow, a punchline waits,
Where roots meet giggles, forming fates!

Sunbeams tickle each branch and bud,
As laughter echoes from the mud.
The leaves join in a vibrant tease,
Filling the air with light, sweet breeze!

Under the trees, we find our muse,
In this world, there's naught to lose.
For in the whispers, joy abounds,
With nature's humor all around!

Branching Out

In the garden, roots do sprout,
With laughter swirling all about.
The plants conspire, it's a hoot,
Tickling toes, oh how they scoot!

Beneath the leaves, a dance of glee,
Weaving tales of birds and bees.
The sun plays tricks, a mischievous light,
While shadows giggle, taking flight.

Vines encroach with a playful tease,
Hiding secrets among the trees.
Nature's joke, a funny route,
Let's not fret, just branch out.

In tangled knots, we find our way,
With every twist, a brighter day.
So join the dance, take a bow,
In this green kingdom, here and now.

Whispers in the Earth

Beneath the soil, the critters chat,
With wriggles and giggles, how about that?
The ants gossip, in fierce debate,
While worms just wiggle, feeling great!

The roots entwined, their stories blend,
"Oh, look at that," the daisies bend.
Underneath the leafy scene,
Who knew the earth could be so keen?

A mushroom's giggle, a beetle's cheer,
Each underground tale brings us near.
In the humus, laughter mingles,
With every wiggle, nature jingles.

A hidden realm where soil thrives,
With snickers and chuckles, life survives.
So next you dig, lend an ear,
You'll hear the laughter, loud and clear.

Life Beneath the Bark

Under the bark, a world of fun,
Beetles and bugs, a wild run.
The squirrels chat and give a cheer,
As creatures plot with no real fear.

A woodpecker knocks, it's quite the show,
"Join our party, come on, let's go!"
Sap drips like laughter, sticky and bright,
In the shade where critters unite.

The fungi whisper, "What's the plan?"
While lichens giggle, "I'm your fan!"
In this wooden party, all is grand,
Each tiny life the fun in hand.

So give a knock on that old oak's side,
Unlock the jokes that bark can hide.
Beneath the crust, we all can see,
Life is a jest; just come and be free.

Understory Chronicles

In the understory, tales unfold,
With leaves above, wild stories told.
The rabbits gossip, the ferns inspire,
As fireflies dance around the pyre.

Mossy carpets, soft and green,
Where humor blooms, if you know what I mean.
A tangle of vines, a comical twist,
Praise to the laughter, we can't resist.

A chattering chipmunk shares a quip,
While shadows sway and branches skip.
In this realm, the air is light,
Each chuckle binds the day to night.

So tiptoe softly through this space,
Join in the fun and keep the pace.
In the understory, come take a seat,
Where every heartbeat holds a beat!

Beneath the Surface

Beneath the soil, things twist and twine,
Wiggly wonders, a radish line.
Roots doing yoga, a leafy ballet,
Dancing through dirt, in a quirky display.

Worms hold meetings, in secretive style,
Plotting to sneak in a garden a while.
With a shovel in hand, they scurry away,
Making mud pies, come join the play!

Under the surface, the laughter does grow,
A root vegetable party, a funny show.
Join in the fun, let yourself unwind,
Where humor sprouts free, and smiles are entwined.

Veins of Thought

In the veins of a plant, ideas flow,
Tickling the leaves with a funny little glow.
Thoughts in a tangle, like noodles in soup,
Bouncing around in a brainy troop.

Photosynthesizing, a joke in the sun,
Leaves crack up, oh isn't this fun?
A silly debate on who's greener than green,
Puns from the petals, you've never seen!

Veins carry whispers, of jokes planted deep,
While flowers snicker and pollen will leap.
Join in the chatter, add to the feast,
Where laughter is shared, nature's joyful beast.

Network of Stanzas

In a network of stanzas, words take a spin,
Rhyme schemes are frolicking, let the fun begin!
A pun serves the punchline, laughter will bloom,
    Metaphors giggle, sharing all the room.

Each verse a vine, interlaced and entwined,
    Weaving together, an endearing bind.
Playful like rabbits, they hop and they skip,
    Making sure humor's never a blip.

Syllables dance on a breeze filled with cheer,
As sonnets and limericks gather round here.
Join in the rhyme, let your worries unlace,
In this jumbled garden, there's plenty of space.

Harmony of Roots

Roots sing a tune in a subterranean band,
With each little bump, they share a grand stand.
Tickled by raindrops, they giggle in glee,
A symphony funky, nature's jubilee.

In harmony strung with a minimal fuss,
The underground jam gets a bit much for us.
Roots sport their jazz hats, they shuffle and sway,
Making mud pies near fungus buffet.

Singing together, they build up their pride,
A rooty rendition, take it all in stride.
In a world underground where the fun never quits,
Join in the laughter, let your roots have glitz!

Garden of Words

In the garden where words grow,
They dance and sway, putting on a show.
Puns blossom like wild daisies bright,
Tickling your mind with pure delight.

Silly sentences sprout in a row,
Comedy blooms, and laughter will flow.
Jokes take root in the soil of the page,
Growing up tall like a wise old sage.

Underground Sonnet

Beneath the surface where whispers creep,
A sonnet is buried, but never asleep.
With rhymes intertwined like roots in the dark,
Silly verses giggle, ready to spark.

Worms write their poems without a care,
In a squiggly script, it's quite rare.
Their ink is the soil; their laughter is deep,
Turning mundane moments to treasures we keep.

Ancestral Echoes

Old words echo from the past, so sly,
Whispering secrets, oh my, oh my!
Grandma's giggles in metaphors bloom,
Her funny stories light up every room.

Ancestors conspire with tales of old,
Turning frowns into laughter, pure gold.
In the family tree, humor takes flight,
Branching out wide in the soft moonlight.

Bursting from the Earth

From the ground sprouts a joke, oh what glee,
A punchline peeks out, just wait and see!
Laughter erupts like flowers in spring,
As humor bursts forth, oh what joy it brings.

Roots may twist in an odd little dance,
Making us chuckle, given the chance.
With each silly rhyme, we surely can hear,
The earth itself giggling, loud and clear.

Subterranean Sonnet

In the soil where secrets creep,
Worms wiggle, plot, and scheme.
A garden party's on the cheap,
Nature's wild but has a dream.

The carrots wear a funky hat,
While radishes dance on their toes.
A beet is playing with a cat,
Who's too busy chasing mows.

Snap peas gossip, green and bold,
While onions blush beneath the sun.
With stories funny, strange, and old,
They giggle till the day is done.

Underneath all that we see,
Lies humor that we can't unearth.
These roots of joy, so wild and free,
Grow laughter deep within the earth.

Veins of Verse

Amid the vines, the words entwine,
Like silly socks that do a dance.
A grape's a poet, can't confine,
To laughter's silly, juicy chance.

The rhymes are grapes that tend to squish,
They pop and giggle with delight.
Some bloom like flowers with a wish,
To make the dreary days feel bright.

A pumpkin boasts a folly bold,
He tells bad jokes, but they're quite sweet.
In this patch, all stories told,
Are rollicking rhymes beneath our feet.

So if you wander through this grove,
Prepare for puns and jests galore.
In every root, a joke will rove,
To tickle hearts forevermore.

Crossroads of Creation

At the corners where thoughts converge,
Ideas sprout like daisies bright.
A mishmash plan, they all emerge,
With giggles dancing in the light.

One sprout suggests a hat parade,
While others try an acorn race.
A patch of wildness, unafraid,
Turns serious tales into a chase.

They trade their seeds for silly dreams,
With shortcuts found in roots and vines.
Each twist and turn can bring more schemes,
As laughter spills like splendid wines.

When paths collide, what will appear?
A curious mix of all that's fun.
In every laugh, the heart can cheer,
In tangled joy, we all are one.

The Rooted Melody

In the deep the tones all hum,
A rhythm found beneath the ground.
With burbling brooks and ants that drum,
Nature's band plays all around.

The roots compose their secret show,
With laughter swirling in the breeze.
More hilarious than we could know,
Their songs bring us to trembling knees.

Each note a sprout, each chord a bloom,
Together mixed in joyous cheer.
A raucous laugh breaks through the gloom,
With every tickle, life draws near.

So dance along this earthy tune,
With roots that wiggle in delight.
For in this place, beneath the moon,
The melody keeps dreams alight.

Patchwork of Poetry

In the garden, words grow wide,
Like a patchwork quilt, side by side.
Each line a whimsy, silly and spry,
Chasing the clouds as they float by.

Bumblebees buzzing, words take flight,
Tickling the toes of the morning light.
Puns blossom brightly, petals unfurl,
A riot of laughter, a poet's whirl.

Nature's Hidden Prose

Under the leaves, a story's told,
By squirrels and shadows, both brave and bold.
They gather acorns, gossip in rhyme,
While ants march in line, keeping good time.

The wind whispers secrets, a tickle or tease,
As daisies wink softly, swaying with ease.
A turtle slips past, in slow-motion jest,
In this tangled tale, we find humor's rest.

Bedrock of Ideas

On mountains of thought, we stumble and trip,
With rocks of odd notions that give us a grip.
Laughter erupts like springs from the earth,
Ideas take flight, for what they're worth.

The boulders resemble the quirks in our minds,
A wacky assortment, of all different kinds.
With each clumsy tumble, we giggle and cheer,
Building our castles, with echoes of beer.

Life's Interconnected Verses

In a tangled web, our thoughts entwine,
Like spaghetti noodles tossed with a brine.
Each bite more zany, a savory jest,
As flavors blend in a whimsical fest.

Life's like a puzzle, funny and bright,
With pieces that jiggle, morning to night.
Amidst all the chaos, we find our own beat,
With laughter as melody, making life sweet.

Depths of Dialogue

In the garden, whispers bloom,
Plants gossip 'neath the moon.
Worms debating root and seed,
Chattering in pulse, they lead.

Beneath the shades, a turtle talks,
To sneaky moles with clever knocks.
Squirrels chime in with laughter bright,
As roots entwine, they share the night.

They're plotting pranks and silly schemes,
Like planting flowers that burst at seams.
The daisies giggle, sunflowers cheer,
In this chatty world, all is clear!

With every twist and turn they weave,
Jokes unfold in what they leave.
Underneath, the stories blend,
A riot blooms without an end.

In the Layered Ground

Underfoot, the chatter's loud,
Among the roots, they form a crowd.
Ants with plans to build a crib,
Dancing crickets, giving a rib.

Mushrooms poke with quirky grace,
Waving fungi, join the race.
Each little sprout has tales to tell,
In this cozy underground shell.

Rats refine their cooking skills,
Spices found among the gills.
While beetles boast of wild escapes,
Turning soil into funny shapes.

Highlights of life beneath the ground,
Where all the joy and laughs abound.
A world of giggles, puns, and cheers,
Sprouting memories through the years.

Nature's Confluence

Streams of chuckles flow and blend,
As branches wave and twigs extend.
The wind delivers silly news,
To flowers dressed in vibrant hues.

Once a leaf, now a paper plane,
Drifting on a giggly gain.
Rabbits dancing with delight,
Through the meadows, taking flight.

Bees do buzz about their fame,
Sharing tales of pollen game.
While frogs croak in jovial tunes,
Underneath the brightened moons.

Together they weave a merry song,
In this wild world, where all belong.
At every turn, joy does abound,
In nature's web, laughter is found.

Folding into the Foliage

Leaves in laughter, shadows play,
Squirrels leap and then delay.
In the brush, a chipmunk grins,
Daring winds to take a spin.

Twisting vines have jokes to share,
Telling tales of sneaky hair.
While bees hum sweet melodies,
Gathering smiles on summer's breeze.

Beneath the boughs, the fun is rife,
Concealed antics, garden life.
A comedy in green attire,
Nature's jesters never tire.

With every rustle, giggles grow,
As breezy friends come out to show.
They fold into the leafy crowd,
With laughter bright and joy unbowed.

The Hidden Network

In the garden, roots do weave,
One tickles toes, I can't believe!
The carrots giggle, the beets all grin,
As the radishes plot, where to begin.

A web of laughter, out of sight,
As veggies dance in pure delight.
Paths crisscross in a sneaky way,
While rabbits hop and squirrels play.

The onions share their secret tales,
While lettuce laughs at veggie fails.
With whispers low, and playful ways,
They plot their pranks for sunny days.

Branching Verses

Down below, things start to play,
Branches wibble, wobble, sway.
The roots form lines like silly mimes,
Drumming beats in hidden climes.

With every twist, they find a chore,
Jokes exchanged like never before.
A tangle here, a tangle there,
They giggle soft in the muddy air.

Whimsical talks, those roots adore,
As beetles tap, they ask for more.
In this game where none can see,
The fun unfolds beneath the lea.

Beneath the Surface

What lies beneath is quite a jest,
Where fungi play their hidden quest.
The dewdrops laugh in every nook,
While earthworms read their latest book.

The mushrooms toss their caps around,
In an underground merry-go-round.
They trip on roots, but never fall,
In their secret world, they have a ball.

With each soft giggle, the soil shakes,
As laughter bubbles, the garden wakes.
In the muddy depths, where few would go,
Silly secrets put on a show.

Entangled Riddles

Two roots met, they shared a pun,
Said one to the other, "Let's have some fun!"
They twisted tight, a playful knot,
In riddled laughs, they forgot their spot.

Behind the leaves, the laughter grew,
As vines debated who knows who.
Cabbage laughed at broccoli's hat,
While peas rolled out—imagine that!

They tell their truths through rhyming vines,
With every turn, their humor shines.
In a garden filled with quirks and cheer,
The roots connect, and jokes appear.

Fragments of Connection

In the garden of giggles, we sprout,
With roots that are tangled, no doubt.
A worm in a tie shows up for tea,
Shouting to daisies, "Come chat with me!"

The daisies reply with a playful cheer,
"Why not share a drink? It's quite sincere!"
They clink little cups made of green blades,
In the midst of their laughter, no need for charades.

Through the grass hops a frog with a hat,
He croaks funny jokes; can you imagine that?
The earth holds their secrets, mud paths unwind,
In the laughter of sprouts, true joy you will find.

As whispers of sweetness drift through the air,
A dance of creation, a curious flair.
Insects don costumes, parade through the mire,
Every chuckle ignites a new spark of fire.

Bound by Soil

Underneath the surface, the roots all meet,
A family of fungi sharing some treats.
With toast made of dirt and a sprinkle of dew,
They feast on the gossip, as deep fables brew.

A leaf holds a grudge, but the soil knows best,
It softens the clash, lets grievances rest.
While beetles debate on their hefty fine,
A ladybug giggles, "It's not yours, it's mine!"

The moles make a ruckus, feeling quite sly,
They're drawn to the fun like a pie in the sky.
"Now who hid my shovel? It was here a minute!"
They dig and they laugh, in playful mischief, you're in it.

In the womb of the earth, they tell silly tales,
Of veggie adventures and treasure trails.
Bound by the soil, let the humor roll free,
In this quirky community, everyone's glee.

Sprouts of Silence

Quietly creeping, the plants sway and bend,
In whispers of chlorophyll, secrets they send.
A shush from the cabbage, a giggle from beans,
While spinach debates with the sweet tangerines.

The onions hold meetings, all layered with thought,
While peas tell tall tales, oh the fun they have sought.
They smile at the sun, who shines ever bright,
Cracking up roots in the dead of the night.

The carrots, though buried, have stories to share,
Of rabbits that tickle, and clouds made of air.
With every sweet sprout, a chuckle takes flight,
In the stillness of green, it's a riotous night.

So under the moonlight, they dance in delight,
Strange friends bound together, a zany sight.
Amidst the stillness, their bond's pure and clear,
In silence, they sprout; oh, how they endear!

Ancestral Ascent

From the roots of the past, a tapestry flows,
With ancestors chuckling in rows and in throes.
Each sprout calls out names of the wise and the bold,
In the laughter of leaves, their legends unfold.

An elder tree holds a council of bugs,
Retelling the tales of their celebratory hugs.
"Remember that time a squirrel stole the show?"
The laughter erupts; the branches all glow.

They weave through the ages with giggles galore,
With acorns that bounce like they're wanting to floor.
A punchline from pine cones gives way to a glee,
As roots drape in memory, sweet history.

Through heights of ascent, and with width unconfined,
They grow with the humor that's shared and combined.
In the whispering woods where the funny ones roam,
Together they flourish, a laughter-filled home.

Nature's Chorus

In the garden, bugs take flight,
Dancing leaves in morning light.
Worms throw parties underground,
Where giggles of the roots are found.

Bees wear hats made out of fluff,
Sipping nectar, oh so tough.
Grass blades whisper silly jokes,
While daisies tease the lazy folks.

Trees gossip with the passing breeze,
Sharing secrets with such ease.
Lizards sing in lizard tunes,
Underneath the watchful moons.

Nature's humor, wild and free,
Tickles plants and bumbles bees.
Every leaf a chuckling chap,
In this verdant, joyous lap.

Hidden Threads

Beneath the soil, a ruckus reigns,
Critters play their silly games.
Fungi dance in shades of green,
Wiggly roots are quite the scene.

Spiders spin their webs of cheer,
Tickling toes that wander near.
Tangled tales of vines unfold,
Mysteries in the soil hold.

Mice debate the best foraging tips,
As snails take leisurely trips.
Lively whispers in the dark,
Set the stage for life's great park.

Every crevice has a laugh,
Nature's wit, a playful craft.
In the underground so grand,
Funny secrets, hand in hand.

Soilbound Song

Oh, plants that hum a merry tune,
With roots that wiggle under moon.
Beets throw parties, dressed in red,
While carrots dance on leafy bed.

A sunflower's hat is big and bright,
Boasting tales of day and night.
With burly weeds playing the fool,
Ripping off the garden rule.

Caterpillars trade their dreams,
For a chance at leafy schemes.
Every sprout has something funny,
In this world of soil and sunny.

Nature sings in chuckles soft,
Tickling the sky, oh so loft.
Soilbound song, so sweet, so wild,
Like laughter of a blooming child.

Rhythms of Growth

In the dance of days gone by,
Worms tap toes and clouds fly high.
Each sprout a dancer in the sun,
Tickled roots just love the fun.

Silly leaves with floppy moves,
Turning rhythms into grooves.
Rabbits giggle, hopping round,
In this bright and playful ground.

Nuts join in with acorn beats,
While beetles glide on tiny seats.
Nature's laughter fills the air,
Tickles roots with loving care.

Growth's a party, wild and bold,
Stories in the blooms unfold.
Every color, every sound,
In this joyous life unbound.

Subterranean Songs

In the soil where secrets twine,
Worms hold court, sipping wine.
Roots tap dance below the grass,
While mushrooms giggle as they pass.

Toadstools wear their hats askew,
A party where the grass is dew.
The beetles play their tiny drums,
As laughter bubbles, joy becomes.

Squirrels gossip about the trees,
While bumblebees hum, buzzing flees.
Vines twist round like a jolly dare,
In a world that thrives on clever flair.

And as the night begins to fade,
Glowworms join the grand charade.
Each root and shoot, a tale to spin,
In underground, where laughs begin.

Flourishing Connections

Creeping vines weave an embrace,
Champignon hats dance with grace.
Laughter echoes in leafy snicker,
As daisies track time, getting thicker.

Silly critters play hide and seek,
Beneath the ferns, the laughter peaks.
Each root entwined, a quirk to share,
In this tangled web without a care.

Tangled up in horticultural fun,
Where even weeds can't help but run.
Bounce to the beat of tiny feet,
As garden gnomes begin to greet.

A willow waves with a happy nod,
While rabbits dance on the grassy plod.
In this merry maze, joy's unrolled,
Where laughs sprout freely, pure and bold.

Entwined Expressions

A tangled tale of roots and leaves,
Causing giggles, laughter weaves.
With mushrooms telling knock-knock jokes,
While snails shout back, 'We're not folks!'

The daisies gossip, pink and white,
About the rogue weeds in their plight.
Twisting stems in a dance routine,
While ladybugs cheer, cute and green.

Caterpillars in a conga line,
Marching through the garden, feeling fine.
Their laughter flits from leaf to flower,
As pollination's the magic power.

Roots are plotting with a wink,
Underneath where no one thinks.
They scheme and dream of leafy flights,
In this green world of funny sights.

Lattice of Lines

A lattice spreads as laughter blooms,
With hairy bugs in tiny rooms.
Each sprout a story, each leaf a jest,
In nature's madness, we're all blessed.

Fronds unfurl with a giggly grin,
Brushing past where laughter's been.
Twine up high, a merry knot,
While shadow games leave laughs in spot.

Funky roots in a tangled play,
Twisting jokes that sway and sway.
Even worms wear silly hats,
As butterflies twirl in joyful spats.

So here's to laughter, deep and wide,
In every nook where jests can hide.
A lattice built on jokes and fun,
In nature's web, we all have won.

Veiled Vignettes

In a garden of giggles, we sprout,
Where plants wear hats, with no doubt.
Chasing shadows, the squirrels all prance,
Doing the tango, in leafy romance.

Bees buzz in rhythm, a quirky ballet,
As flowers tell jokes in their flowery way.
Petunias wear glasses, act all aloof,
But the daisies just laugh, swinging from the roof.

Mice in the meadow are plotting a play,
With carrots for props, they rehearse every day.
The sun shines bright, a spotlight so grand,
While butterflies flutter, a fan club on hand.

The wind whispers secrets, a mischievous breeze,
While tomatoes gossip, and giggle with ease.
Nature's a stage, in this comical rhyme,
Let's laugh through the seasons, one leaf at a time.

Buried Echoes

In a land of lost shoes, where socks go to hide,
Echoes of laughter, they cannot abide.
A shifty old fox holds a treasure map tight,
But it's full of nonsense, a real silly sight.

The worms hold a party, beneath the warm ground,
With radishes dancing, all spinning around.
"Dig deeper!" they cheer, for an underground feast,
While ants bring the snacks, it's a buggy kind beast.

Toads croak old songs, with a wobbly beat,
Each note makes the others bounce on their feet.
The moon rolls its eyes, oh what a delight,
While shadows chuckle at the silliest sight.

But when morning comes knocking, they hide in the shade,
For laughter is best when it's cleverly played.
The echoes of chuckles that linger and sway,
Remind us of fun in the quirkiest way.

Crossroads of Poetry

Where words stumble, and puns like to roam,
At the junction of verses, we find our true home.
A signpost says, "Left for the really bad jokes,"
While right leads to laughter, with giggling folks.

A cat in a hat, singing songs of delight,
With a parrot named Bob, who just loves to bite.
They dance on the pavement, in splendid array,
While the owls keep watch, in a fun-loving sway.

Bards come a-running, with quills in their hands,
To scribble the madness that no one understands.
The air is electric, with wit on the breeze,
As the trees start to chuckle, with their rustling leaves.

So come take a turn at this whimsical way,
Where the silly and serious play every day.
At the crossroads of all, where the humor takes flight,
Join the merry band in this comical night.

Tapestry of Life

Woven together, the stories unfold,
With threads made of laughter, and colors quite bold.
The cats play chess, while the dogs spin a tale,
Of unicorns who sail on ships made of kale.

Socks talk in whispers, about their lost mates,
While spoons share secrets of their dinner plate dates.
The bread rolls around, doing flips in the air,
Creating a show that's deliciously rare.

The sun beams a spotlight on all that we share,
As clouds float on by, without a single care.
A tapestry vibrant, filled with every jest,
Each stitch crafted gently, as we all feel blessed.

So weave in your laughs, let your spirit run free,
In this funny old world, just come join the spree.
For life is a quilt, stitched with joy and with strife,
And we're all just the threads, in this tapestry of life.

The Tapestry of Roots

In gardens where the veggies play,
Carrots dance a jig each day.
Beans and peas join in the fun,
Under the warm and shining sun.

Tomatoes giggle, ripe and round,
While radishes spin on squishy ground.
Each sprout with tales they love to tell,
In this patch, all's fun and well.

With roots entwined, they plot and scheme,
A leafy choir, a vibrant dream.
Pulling pranks beneath the soil,
In their world, there's no toil.

Among the dirt, they play and thrive,
Singing songs, oh how they jive!
Life underground's a riotous feast,
Nature's jesters, to say the least.

Chords of Coalescence

In the garden where we meet,
Every weed has tap dancing feet.
They sway to the roots' funky beat,
While the flowers twirl, oh so sweet.

The carrots whisper secrets low,
While turnips form a funky show.
Invisible links keep them tight,
In the soil, they dance all night.

Bumping into bugs, what a sight!
Each beetle's joke, a pure delight.
Laughing leaves with giggly tones,
Meet the roots, their hidden bones.

Underneath where shadows lay,
Laughter rumbles, come what may.
Roots connect in joyful glee,
Creating fun for you and me.

Rooted Verses

In tangled beds where laughter grows,
Mischievous sprouts strike silly poses.
A broccoli wears a tiny hat,
While peas play chess with a playful cat.

Radishes giggle, rolling down,
As pumpkins sport a vibrant frown.
All while herbs share spicy tales,
About the time they sailed in gales.

Each root a story, bold and bright,
Whispering secrets in the night.
Through earthy paths, they draw a map,
For curious critters, a joyful trap.

In this laughter, life's a jest,
Nature's way, simply the best.
Roots and rhymes entwined in cheer,
A fun-filled world, forever near.

Tangled Echoes

In gardens dense, where laughter roams,
Daffodils create their homes.
They sing of soil with giggling grace,
While worms join in, a wiggly race.

Underneath, where shadows creep,
Roots conspire, secrets to keep.
The daisies toss their heads so high,
While beetles buzz and butterflies fly.

They tickle the ground, a playful game,
Cucumbers prank with no one to blame.
This underworld, a funny plot,
Nature's circus, like it or not.

Connected by whispers barely heard,
A rooty chat, absurdly absurd.
In this fun, together they weave,
A tapestry of giggles, we believe.

Roots of Resonance

In the garden, a dance so spry,
Wiggly roots, oh my, oh my!
They gossip and giggle, in soil's embrace,
Chasing their dreams at a rapid pace.

Worms tell tales, with a wiggle and twist,
Of secret adventures, none can resist.
With carrots wearing wigs and lettuce in shoes,
They throw silent parties, gathering clues.

Dandelions laugh at their neighbors' fears,
As they blow out wishes and giggles like cheers.
While radishes scamper to play hide and seek,
Being rooty and nutty, they're all quite unique.

So next time you wander through green leafy lanes,
Remember the laughter beneath in the gains.
For roots have a way of connecting the fun,
In their underground dance, they never are done.

Underground Whispers

Beneath the soil, secrets do flow,
Where veggies and critters begin their show.
A radish whispers, 'Did you see that?'
While onions giggle, 'Let's all wear a hat!'

The carrots compete in a hopscotch spree,
While moles compose music, under a tree.
With rhythm and rhymes, they chatter and cheer,
Their funny antics, forever sincere.

Potatoes roll in, all muddy and bright,
Saying, 'Join our party, it's such a delight!'
The peas pop up, in their pods they convene,
Singing of happiness, peaceful and green.

What stories they share, in their cozy embrace,
Of mishaps and giggles that tickle and trace.
Remember, my friend, when you garden tonight,
The underground whispers, will give you delight!

Tangles of Thought

In a patch of green, thoughts twist and shout,
Rooted in laughter, they dance about.
Tangled and jumbled, ideas intertwine,
Like vines that crank up the comedy line.

The beet laughs loudly, 'I'm redder than you!'
While mint sips tea, in the shade, feeling blue.
As pumpkins debate their roundness and size,
Their bumpy discussions become quite the surprise.

Tomatoes with glasses, reading the news,
'What's growing on? Oh, we have the blues!'
As peppers critique the flavor of pie,
A cabbage retorts, 'I just wish I could fly!'

So let's not forget, in this garden of glee,
The tangled of thoughts set the mind free.
With humor as vibrant as nature's own hue,
Join in the mirth—in this life, it's all true!

Interwoven Echoes

Between the roots, echoes giggle and hum,
In the soil where the squishy things come.
A chorus of laughter, a raucous team,
Where the tiny bugs join in a dream.

The mushrooms discuss their favorite jokes,
While beetles roll by, doing flips and pokes.
With flowers that sway, oh, what a sight,
Swaying and dancing, they bring pure delight.

In the cool of the evening, the radishes sing,
Celebrating the joy that a garden can bring.
While critters parade, with costumes galore,
Interwoven echoes, a festival roar.

So let's tip our hats to this merry crew,
With roots linking laughter in every hue.
For nature knows well, in silly repose,
The best kind of joy, always grows and grows!

Underground Melodies

In the soil where fungi play,
Tiny critters dance all day.
With roots that twist and roots that twirl,
They whisper secrets to the girl.

Worms giggle as they wiggle by,
While ants march on with a tie.
Leaves drop tunes to the earth below,
In a concert where the wild things grow.

Mice with hats and little boots,
Tap their toes to some rooty flutes.
Grass blades sway to the funky beat,
As mushrooms groovy move their feet.

What a jam beneath our feet!
Roots and rhymes, oh what a treat!
A garden party, all aglow,
With laughter shared, they steal the show.

Interwoven Whispers

In tangled webs where secrets dwell,
Gossipy roots have tales to tell.
Under the grass, a party grows,
With jokes that only a beetle knows.

Squirrels giggle, tails in knots,
Sharing gossip from the plots.
With little seeds that sprout and pop,
Funny stories never stop!

Caterpillars with hats so grand,
Scoff at the town of shifting sand.
Dandelions blowing thoughts of cheer,
Who knew the underground had such a sphere?

Beneath the surface, life gets rowdy,
With tunes that make the earth feel cloudy.
Interwoven jokes and laughs abound,
In the garden, joy is always found!

Mycelium Musings

Beneath the dirt, a network sprawls,
A fungi party with funny calls.
Mushrooms giggling, tipping their caps,
While beetles share their midday naps.

With wisdom held in spongy threads,
They ponder life and mix their breads.
Toasts with truffles, oh what a feast,
As critters laugh, they thrive at least!

With every twist and play of fate,
Connections bloom, oh isn't it great?
In mycelium dreams, they plot and scheme,
Life's a comedy, or so it would seem.

So if you wander down the lane,
And hear the laughter, don't refrain.
Join the fungi, it's quite a scene,
Where humor grows, and nothing's routine!

Branching Narratives

Through branches thick and twigs so thin,
Stories unfold like a win-win grin.
Chirping birds share tales of fun,
While squirrels scamper, always on the run.

Laughter echoes from tree to tree,
As branches wave in harmony.
"Did you see the acorn fall?"
It sparked a giggle, a squirrel's call.

Under the canopy, stories abound,
Where every rustle holds joy profound.
A tale of mischief from dawn till night,
With every twist, the mood feels right!

So climb aboard this leafy ride,
Where humor blossoms, side by side.
Branching out, we share our fates,
In nature's book, where laughter waits!

Twisted Harmonies

In the garden where giggles grow,
Worms wear wigs and put on a show.
Roots entwine in a dance so spry,
While frogs in tuxedos pass by.

The apples debate what color to be,
While carrots complain, "We can't see!"
A cabbage tops the vegetable chart,
And sings to a beet with a big, shiny heart.

Lettuce laughs at the sun's warm rays,
While radishes reminisce on their days.
Underneath, there's a party, it seems,
With belly laughs sprouting from dreams.

In this patch, all is silly and bright,
Where cucumbers twirl in the moonlight.
Growing together, they weave a song,
In twisted harmonies all night long.

Grounded Lyrics

Down in the soil, the puns take root,
Where peas in pods wear their best suit.
A sunflower stands, with a grin so wide,
Bragging of heights, with seeds as its pride.

The onions cry jokes, making everyone laugh,
While potatoes debate their shape and their half.
"Am I a spud, or a round little ball?"
They laugh 'til they tumble, down they all fall.

The carrots are dancing, oh what a sight,
In the glow of the moon, under stars shining bright.
Together they hum a grounding refrain,
Creating a ruckus, no room for disdain.

In this dirt patch, joy's what we find,
With grounded lyrics, the best of its kind.
So join the jive, let your roots intertwine,
As we celebrate laughter, pure and divine.

Networked Rhapsodies

In the web of the wild, a coder's delight,
Digital daisies bloom day and night.
A server of giggles, hosting the fun,
While squirrels upload, and the chatbots run.

Bees buzz tunes in a networked spree,
With flowers commenting, "That's new to me!"
Caterpillars crawl through the data's maze,
Each byte a joke, in a whimsical haze.

Glitches are laughter, and bugs turn to cheer,
In a digital garden where all is sincere.
With each quirky update, we spring up like grass,
These rhapsodies dance with a humorous sass.

So patch in your joy, let's update our song,
In this world of bytes, we all belong.
Networked together, with smiles to share,
In rhapsodies of laughter, we soar through the air.

Veins of Verse

Through the veins of the earth, laughter flows,
As mushrooms tell puns and the lavender glows.
Silly critters peek from beneath every rock,
While squirrels chitter-chatter, they just can't stop!

The thyme gives a wink, and the basil just sighs,
While radishes giggle with bright, bulging eyes.
In this green place, the humor is grand,
With roots that tickle, and vines that expand.

Flowers burst forth in a colorful spree,
Telling tall tales of the bumblebee.
The earth resonates with humor and cheer,
In the veins of verse, there's nothing to fear.

So come join the fun, where jokes never fade,
In this garden of giggles, together we've laid.
With each playful line, our spirits unite,
In the joyous rhythm, we dance through the night.

Burgeoning Voices

In a garden of giggles so spry,
Silly plants reach for the sky.
With vines that twist, oh what a sight,
Marigolds dance in the moonlight.

Dandelions whisper a joke,
While carrots wear shades, oh what a stroke!
Sunflowers sway with a grin so wide,
Nature's laughter can't be denied.

The onions cry tears, but they join in too,
Yelling out puns, as all good friends do.
In this patch of play, the roots intertwine,
Growing together, oh what a fine line!

Earth's Quiet Lyrics

Beneath the surface, the whispers hum,
Roots tickle and laugh, oh how they become!
Twirling in shadows where giggles reside,
Even the soil seems to be amused inside.

A worm writes a sonnet with flair and style,
While fungi perform with a cheeky smile.
Grasshoppers chirp in a rhythmic cheer,
"Life's but a stage, come join us, my dear!"

With each little poke, the earth joins the fun,
Singing along as the day is begun.
In the quiet it echoes, this symphony thrives,
Both silly and clever, it's how nature survives!

Interlaced Dreams

In tangled thoughts where butterflies play,
Dreams interlace like vines in ballet.
A daisy tells tales of its past adventures,
While honeysuckle giggles, feeling the censures.

The lily hops and waves, quite a show,
With roots in a chorus, stealing the glow.
Petals coconuts whisper, share a whole plot,
A comedy script that's twisted in thought.

As shadows interweave in a dance of delight,
Every stitch of whimsy is perfectly tight.
In this garden of jest, all worries take flight,
While dreams weave a tapestry, oh what a sight!

Mystic Roots

Deep in the earth where secrets are kept,
Wise old roots laugh while the world's inept.
With glee they spread wide, sharing the lore,
    Making wisecracks as they explore.

An acorn jokes, "I'll be mighty one day!"
While a sprout ponders the games they will play.
"Let's start a club!" the mushrooms declare,
    In a world of their own, without a care.

Nature's committee, with quirks to spare,
Telling tall tales as they twist in midair.
With laughter beneath, and a chuckle above,
Mystic roots thrive in their patch of love!

Flora's Lament

In the garden where daisies pout,
A gopher has chewed them all out.
With radishes whispering, 'What the heck?'
They giggle at roots that just can't connect.

The tulips complain of the thorny vine,
Who promised to dance but just crossed a line.
While the sunflowers roll their eyes with glee,
'At least we're best buds with the bumblebee!'

The peppers were worried, all wrapped in green,
'Is it fashion or nature? We can't be seen!'
Yet in this patch, the laughter took flight,
As radishes joked about their plight.

With a sigh, Flora sighed, 'It's a wild affair,
In this jumbled jungle, we haven't a care!'
And so they laughed, beneath the moonlight,
In the ruckus of roots, everything felt right.

Unseen Connections

In the soil, secrets twist and twine,
The carrots giggle, feeling just fine.
Beans tell stories through whispers below,
While onions join in with their potent woe.

Underneath, where no one can see,
The mushrooms chuckle, 'We hold the key!'
They trade wisecracks with the vibrant weeds,
And all share laughs like nature's good deeds.

'Why do they walk when they can just grow?'
Chortles the fern, high in the flow.
The vines laugh back, 'Let's dance in the breeze!'
And twirl with the flowers, like swaying trees.

While roots intertwine to build a great tale,
Making the soil a fun, squishy trail.
In the underground party, life's got its perks,
With nature's own magic, confusion lurks.

Dense Canopy Chronicles

In the jungle, the monkeys swing low,
While the vines do a tango, all in a row.
Parrots squawk secrets between the fronds,
A raucous affair, like nature's bonds.

The ferns composed rhymes with such flair,
While lianas looped tales in the air.
From leaf to leaf, giggles spread wide,
Under the canopy, no place to hide!

'Why'd the moth fly into the light?'
A beetle snickers, 'It's quite a sight!'
With roots sipping gossip from puddles nearby,
The fables of foliage just seem to fly.

The rain patters down, providing the beat,
As plants breakdance in nature's own street.
With colors awash, and laughter so bright,
In the dense canopy, all feels just right.

Rooted Symphony

Deep in the earth, a concert unfolds,
Where the carrots play bass, and the radishes hold.
Beets curl away with a jazzy sound,
While the daisies clap, spinning around.

The roots harmonize, strumming low songs,
Reciting the tales that nature prolongs.
While the flowers sway in a cosmic groove,
Rustling leaves make the rhythm improve.

Swinging in harmony, tomatoes delight,
As the beans do the cha-cha into the night.
A pep talk from fungi, 'Do keep it loose!'
Chorusing fungi with flair, they let loose!

And up above, the branches applaud,
Rooted together, not a single façade.
In this rooted symphony, laughter resonates,
As the soil sings loud about pesky mates.

Ephemeral Tendrils

A plant once danced in a pot,
With roots that wriggled a lot.
It twirled and spun, oh what a sight!
It thought it was ready for flight.

The neighbors laughed from their yards,
Seeing plants playing their cards.
They'd cheer, they'd boo with delight,
As the tendril rolled like a kite.

The vine claimed it could sing tunes,
Under the light of silver moons.
Its high notes caught in the breeze,
Tickled the leaves of the trees.

Then came a storm, oh so fierce,
The pot got tossed, it felt pierced.
With a flop and a squash, it fell down,
Now it's the jester of the town.

The tale it tells is a riot,
About trying to start a plant diet.
With each giggle, skip, and leap,
The humor of roots runs deep.

Cartography of Soil

In muddy maps, the earth is drawn,
Where radishes laugh at the dawn.
Carrots dream of a soil parade,
While potatoes throw shade in the glade.

Worms weave roads with their squiggly path,
Charting routes with a gentle laugh.
They giggle as they burrow deep,
Creating chaos beneath their sleep.

The cabbage guards its leafy domain,
A general in a garden campaign.
"Let's march!" it shouts with leafy cheer,
While squashes roll, grinning ear to ear.

The rocks play dead, all stony-faced,
But secretly hope they're not misplaced.
With every seed, the ground erupts,
An underground party, all good lucks!

As the sun sets low on the crest,
The roots high-five, they're truly blessed.
In the soil, there's joy to be found,
In a world where giggles abound.

Woodland Lines

In the woods, a squirrel's rap unfolds,
With acorns three, its stash of golds.
It busts a rhyme on a tree stump stage,
While the owls hoot their wisdom sage.

The branches sway in a merry dance,
While mushrooms pop in a mossy stance.
Each rustle tells a funny tale,
As the critters join in the wild gale.

Foxes, rabbits, they all agree,
That nature's a place to just be free.
A dance-off breaks 'neath the tall pine,
With roots tapping right in time, oh divine!

But watch your step, don't trip a root,
Or you'll find yourself wearing a fruit!
Laughter echoes through the glen,
A woodland scene, alive again.

Pollen in the Breeze

Bees buzz around like a marching band,
With pollen sacks as their grandstand.
They wiggle and jiggle in the sun,
Dancing together, oh what fun!

Flower petals flash their colors bright,
Enticing bees with pure delight.
"Join our party, don't be shy!"
Said the daisies, waving hi!

The wind chuckled as it swept by,
Tickling blooms as it went awry.
"Oh dear," it whispered, "what a sight,
A pollen party, pure delight!"

As the sun began to set low,
The flowers sighed, putting on a show.
With twirling stamen, they made a plea,
"Next time, bring donuts and tea!"

So when you stroll through blossoms fair,
Remember the buzzing, the laughter in air.
For in each breeze, a chuckle's found,
Where pollen dances all around.

Tendrils of Sound

A tickle of laughter escapes from the ground,
Where whispers of giggles perform all around.
The trees wear a grin, their branches a wig,
As squirrels act out in a dance, oh so big.

The wind sings a tune that sways with delight,
While mushrooms are jigging, what a wild sight!
A chorus of crickets play trumpets so loud,
In this wacky concert, we sway with the crowd.

Frogs join the band with a ribbit and croak,
Each note of their symphony sparks up a joke.
With roots as the rhythm, they tap on the earth,
This melody's magic, we all share in mirth.

In this garden of sounds that tickle your ear,
The joy of the roots is perfectly clear.
For every chortle that bubbles and spins,
A giggle from nature is where fun begins.

Fables from the Forest

Once upon a time, a tree started to chat,
To a squirrel with dreams of a top-hat and that!
They spoke of the stars, how they'd make quite the scene,
In the realm of the forest, where all is serene.

A hedgehog with glasses read tales filled with laughs,
Of owls in tuxedos organizing drafts.
The rabbits played poker, their bets made of clover,
In the game of the woods, luck never rolls over.

A raccoon wore a cape, claimed to be a knight,
Guarding acorns at dawn, oh what a sight!
With bark for their armor and pine cones their shields,
Each quest in the forest yields laughter that heals.

And stories that sprout from the roots of old trees,
Bring chuckles to all in the rustling breeze.
So gather, dear friends, let's weave tales with cheer,
In the fables of forest, fun's always near.

Enigmatic Roots

Deep down below, where the shadows reside,
The roots tell their secrets, in whispers, they bide.
They chuckle and giggle, their stories so bold,
Of earthworms who paint with the soil they hold.

There's a kraken of carrots, with legs long and lean,
Who dreams of the ocean, where he's never been seen.
The broccoli crowns gossip, with leaflets so sly,
As they conjure up plots, underneath the blue sky.

In this curious world where the roots like to play,
Each twist and each turn leads to humor's ballet.
The laughter of plants is a symphony sweet,
Growing sideways and up, can't help but tap feet.

So dive into soil, where the giggles ignite,
In the whispers of roots, everything feels right.
Their enigmatic tales wrap the earth tight in glee,
With levity swirling, so wild and so free.

Ethereal Growth

Beneath the moonlight, the blossoms take flight,
With petals like wings, they dance through the night.
They giggle in colors, a vibrant parade,
As the fairies drop jokes from the leaves they have laid.

A daffodil whispers, 'Oh, what a fine breeze!'
While daisies spin tales with such effortless ease.
The onions wear hats made of soil and delight,
In this world of growth, everything's out of sight.

Stars twinkle above, like their own little jest,
As the garden rejoices in nature's own fest.
Each root tells a story with laughter entwined,
Uncovering secrets that tickle the mind.

With spirals of joy that reach up to the sky,
In this world full of whimsy, together we fly.
Ethereal growth is the laughter we find,
In the playful embrace of the wild, unconfined.

www.ingramcontent.com/pod-product-compliance
Lightning Source LLC
Chambersburg PA
CBHW051645160426
43209CB00004B/794